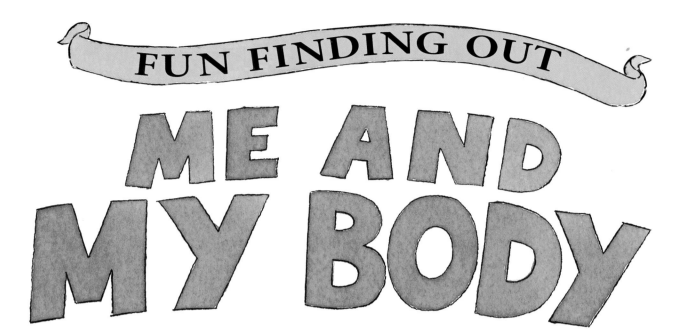

FUN FINDING OUT
ME AND MY BODY

Rosie McCormick   **Anthony Lewis**

KINGƒISHER
NEW YORK

KINGFISHER
Larousse Kingfisher Chambers Inc.
95 Madison Avenue
New York, New York 10016

First published in 1998
10 9 8 7 6 5 4 3 2 (HC)
10 9 8 7 6 5 4 3 2 (PB)
2TR/0699/TWP/FR(FR)/150NYM

LIBRARY OF CONGRESS CATALOGING-IN-PUBLICATION DATA
McCormick, Rosie.
        Me and my body / Rosie McCormick, Anthony Lewis.—
1st ed.
              p.   cm.—(Fun finding out)
        Includes index.
        Summary: A simple introduction to the human body,
discussing its different parts and how they work.
        1. Human anatomy—Juvenile literature.   2. Body, Human—
Juvenile literature.   [1. Body, Human.   2. Human anatomy.]
I. Lewis, Anthony.   II. Title.   III. Series.
QM27.M423   1998   611—dc21   97-39705   CIP AC

ISBN 0-7534-5126-3 (HC)
ISBN 0-7534-5127-1 (PB)

Series editor: Sue Nicholson
Series designer: Kathryn Caulfield
Printed in Singapore

Answers
Staying healthy
1. Drink water; 2. Eat healthy food; 3. Exercise;
4. Get plenty of sleep

Seeing is believing
1. The two lines are the same length—the arrows
on the ends of each line make us think the one
on the left is longer.
2. You may be able to see white arrows AND black
arrows!

Things that help the doctor
Stethoscope—to listen to your breathing or
hear your heart beating; Flashlight—so the doctor
can see into your ears or down your throat;
Thermometer—to take your temperature

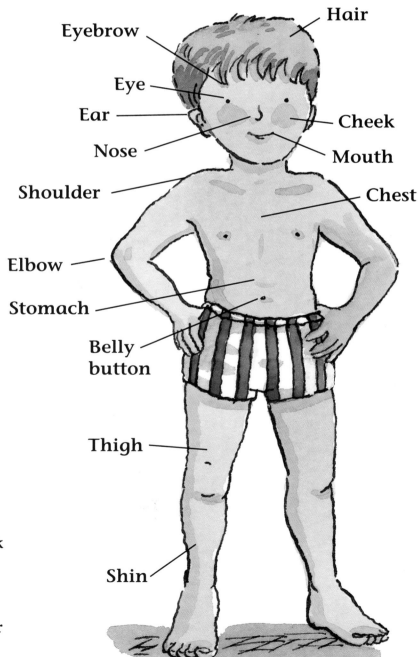

Contents

Fingers

Hand

Arm

Head

Neck

Waist

Hips

Leg

Knee

Ankle

Foot

Toes

My body   4

My muscles and bones   6

My heart and lungs   8

My brain   10

My skin   12

My ears   14

My eyes   16

My nose and tongue   18

My stomach   20

My teeth   22

When I am sick   24

Staying healthy   26

Where I came from   28

Growing up   30

Index   32

My body

The world is full of MILLIONS of people. On the outside, everyone looks different. That makes every single person special—including you! But on the inside, everyone is the same. That's because our bodies are made of the same things and work in the same way.

All kinds of people

People come in all kinds of shapes and sizes, with different-colored hair, eyes, and skin. What do you look like?

We may have different-colored skin.

... or curly hair.

We may have straight hair...

To keep our bodies healthy—both inside and out—we all need to eat good food, drink plenty of water, and get lots of exercise and sleep.

...or short.

We may be tall...

...or small.

We may be large...

What your body needs

What do you need to do to stay healthy?

1

2

3

4

5

My muscles and bones

The bones in your body give you shape and hold you up. Without them, you would fall over like a ragdoll! Bones also protect the softer parts inside your body, such as your brain. Your muscles move your bones around so you can walk, wave, run, and jump.

Your muscles are attached to your bones by strong, stringy bands called tendons.

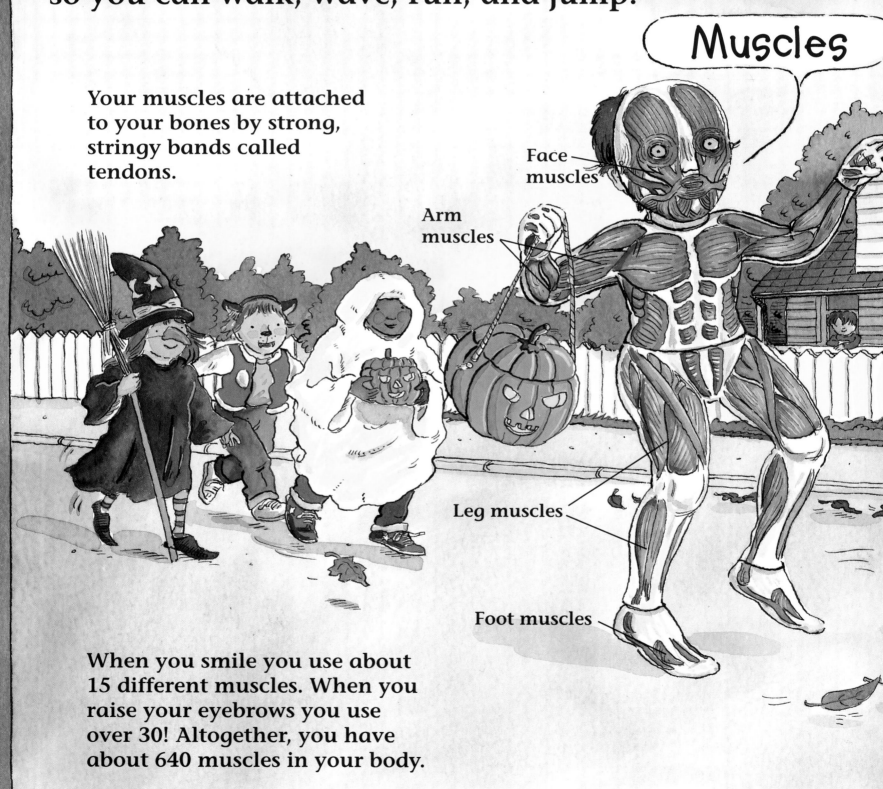

Muscles

Face muscles

Arm muscles

Leg muscles

Foot muscles

When you smile you use about 15 different muscles. When you raise your eyebrows you use over 30! Altogether, you have about 640 muscles in your body.

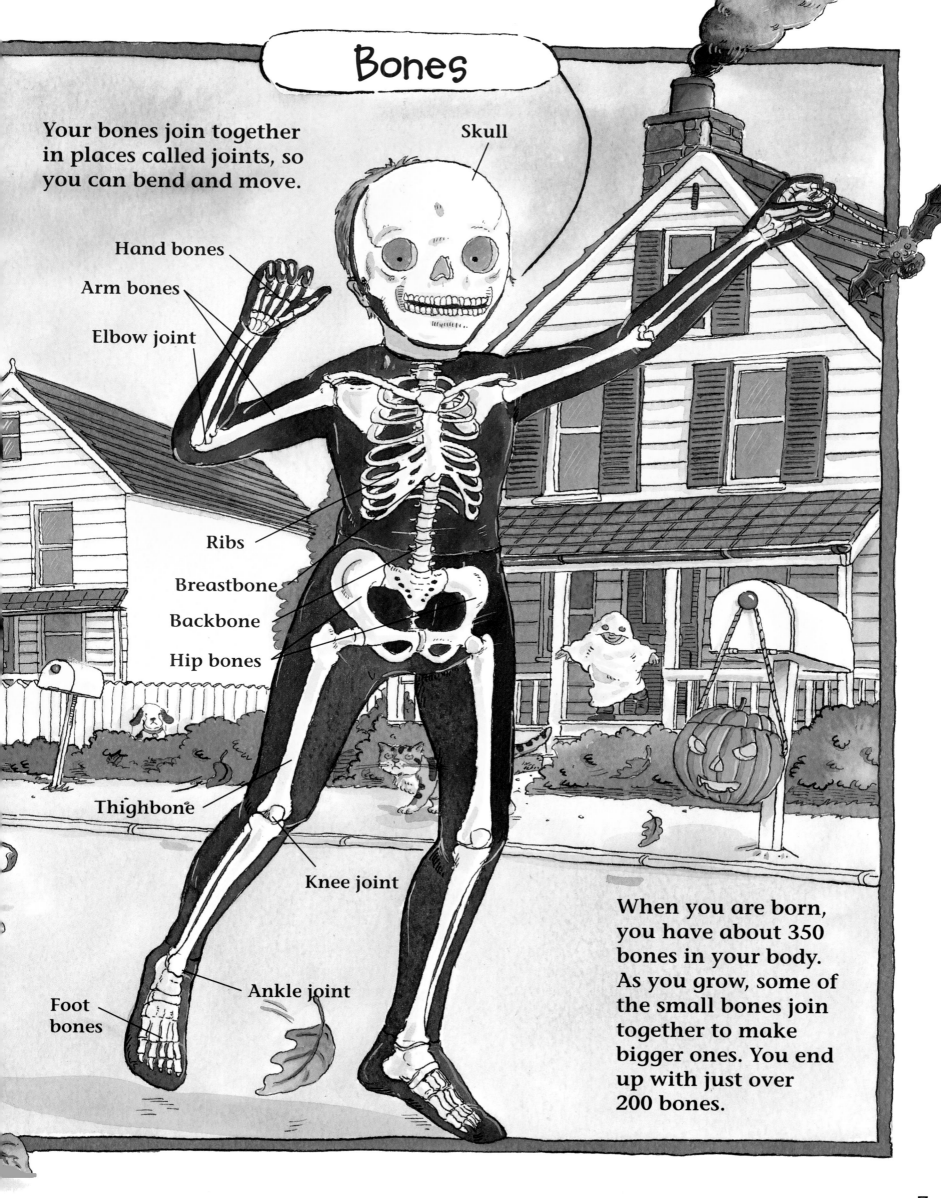

Bones

Your bones join together in places called joints, so you can bend and move.

Skull

Hand bones

Arm bones

Elbow joint

Ribs

Breastbone

Backbone

Hip bones

Thighbone

Knee joint

Ankle joint

Foot bones

When you are born, you have about 350 bones in your body. As you grow, some of the small bones join together to make bigger ones. You end up with just over 200 bones.

My heart and lungs
Thump–thump, thump–thump...

If you touch your chest firmly, you can feel your heart beating. As it beats, your heart is pumping blood all around your body. Your lungs supply your blood with oxygen from the air you breathe.

Sneezing helps keep your nose clear so you can breathe properly. You yawn when your body needs to take in more oxygen.

Your lungs hold the same amount of air as a party balloon. Lungs get bigger when you breathe in and smaller when you breathe out.

When you breathe in, air goes through your nose and mouth and down your windpipe into your lungs. Your body needs oxygen from the air to stay alive.

1 Your heart beats all the time—every second or so. One side of your heart pumps blood to your lungs to get oxygen. The other side pumps blood filled with oxygen all around your body.

2 The blood travels around your body in tiny thin tubes called blood vessels. Blood vessels that carry blood filled with oxygen are called arteries. The ones without oxygen are called veins.

3 Your blood carries oxygen and nourishment from the food you eat to every part of your body. It also helps your body fight germs.

Windpipe

Heart

Lung

Artery

My brain

Inside your head, protected by your skull, is your brain. Your brain is very important because it controls everything you do. It takes in information and sends out signals to the rest of your body, telling it how to work.

Your brain is about half the size of your head. It looks just like a crinkly walnut.

Brain power

Your brain helps you remember things. Look at these pictures, then cover them up. How many can you remember?

Parts of the brain

Your brain is divided into different parts.
Each part has a different job to do.

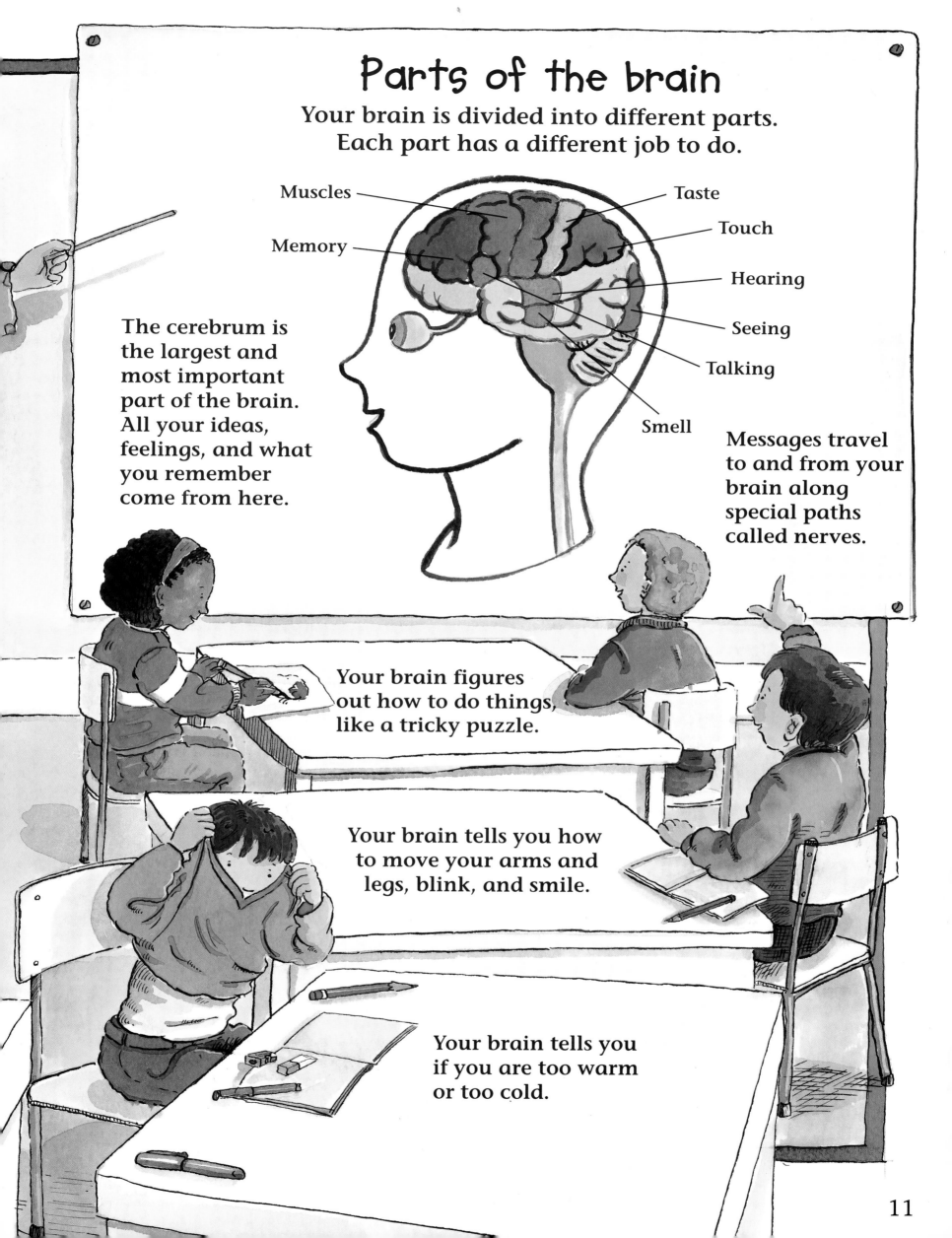

Muscles

Taste

Touch

Memory

Hearing

Seeing

Talking

Smell

The cerebrum is the largest and most important part of the brain. All your ideas, feelings, and what you remember come from here.

Messages travel to and from your brain along special paths called nerves.

Your brain figures out how to do things, like a tricky puzzle.

Your brain tells you how to move your arms and legs, blink, and smile.

Your brain tells you if you are too warm or too cold.

My skin

Your skin is really amazing. It covers your body, from the top of your head to the tips of your toes, and it grows with you as you grow. It protects you from germs and injuries. And it keeps your insides where they should be—inside your body.

Skin is very sensitive to the sun's rays and may get burned. Suntan lotion helps protect it.

The hair on your head also helps protect you from the sun.

Everyone's skin contains a substance called melanin. Melanin is a natural protection from the sun. Dark skin has more melanin than light skin.

Your skin is waterproof. It keeps water from getting into your body.

Healing skin

If you cut yourself, your skin can heal itself.

1 Your blood forms a scab to cover the damaged area.

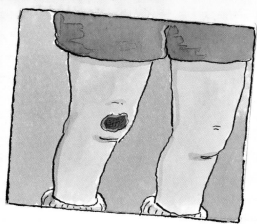

2 New skin starts to grow underneath the scab.

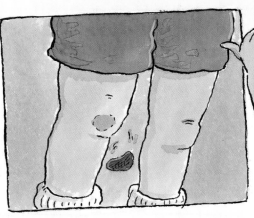

3 When the wound has healed, the scab falls off.

The skin on your fingers and toes is covered in a pattern of tiny swirly lines. These are your fingerprints and toeprints. No one else has the same prints as you.

Underneath your skin are millions of tiny nerves that send out messages to different parts of your body.

Nerves tell your brain whether you are touching something rough or smooth, hot or cold— or whether it hurts!

My ears

Crash, bang, boom!

Your ears can hear all kinds of sounds, from a loud yell to a quiet whisper. Listening to sounds helps us understand what is happening in the world around us.

Besides being able to hear, most people can see, smell, taste, and touch. These are our senses. They allow us to listen to music, read a book, enjoy a tasty meal, or feel a fluffy kitten's fur!

Crash!

Twang

Screech

Toot Toot

Your ears don't just hear sounds, they also help you keep your balance. Inside your ears are special tubes filled with liquid. When you jump around, the liquid moves around, too. As it moves, it sends messages to your brain, letting it know if you need extra help to stay on your feet!

Ding-a-ling

How we hear

Our ears are funnel-shaped to catch sounds from the air.

Tra-la-la

Hammer bone

Nerves carry messages to the brain

Anvil bone

Stirrup bone

Eardrum

Ear

1 Sounds enter your ear and make your eardrum, and the three tiny bones behind it, move back and forth.

2 A liquid deep in your ear moves then, too. Nerves feel this movement and send signals to your brain.

15

My eyes

When it's dark, it's difficult to see. When it's sunny and bright, or when you turn on the light, you can see more clearly. That's because your eyes need light to help them see.

How we see

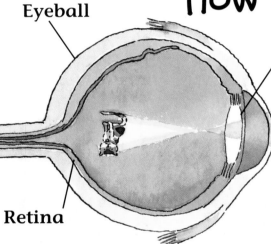

Eyeball

The lens helps your eyes focus.

Retina

Your whole eye is shaped like a ball.

When you look at something, an upside-down picture of it appears on the back of your eyeball. Nerves send a message about the picture to your brain, and your brain turns it right-side up.

Seeing is believing

Sometimes our eyes play tricks on us. Look at these pictures.

Which line is longer?

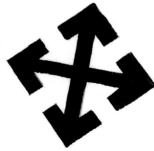

Are the arrows black or white?

16

Light and dark

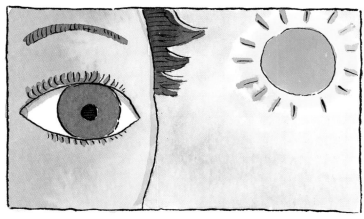

In bright light, your pupils become smaller so they don't take in too much light and dazzle you.

In dim light, your pupils become larger so they can take in more light and you can see better.

Eyebrow
Eyelid
Pupil
Iris
Eyelash
Tear duct

Eyebrows keep drops of sweat out of your eyes. Eyelashes keep dust and dirt from getting into them, and tear ducts help keep them clean. The iris is the colored part of your eye.

Some people need a little extra help to see correctly, so they wear glasses.

My nose and tongue

Your nose helps you smell things, such as a smelly drain, or a sweetly-scented flower. Your tongue helps you taste things, such as delicious chocolate ice cream. It also helps you talk and sing.

Smelly fish

Strong-smelling cheese

Stinky garbage c

Bitter

Sour and salty

Sweet

Your tongue is covered with lots of tiny bumps called taste buds. Taste buds on different parts of your tongue pick up strong tastes.

You taste bitter things on the back of your tongue, sour and salty things at the sides, and sweet things on the tip.

Smoky fumes

Sweet-smelling flowers

NY

"Hello"

Find out how important your tongue is for talking. Hold the tip of your tongue between your thumb and index finger and try to say "hello." Can you say it clearly?

When you have a cold your nose sometimes gets stuffed up. This stops you from smelling—and enjoying—your food.

Stinky drains

Your sense of smell is *much* stronger than your sense of taste. Without it, it is hard to taste your food. Try holding your nose when you eat a tasty snack. Can you taste it?

My stomach

Munch, munch, crunch!

After you have smelled, tasted, and chewed your food, you swallow it. The food then travels through long winding pipes and tubes—all the way from your mouth to your bottom.

1 First, the food travels down a food pipe called the gullet. When it reaches your stomach it is squashed and mashed into a pulpy soup.

2 The pulp is then squeezed through a long winding tube called the intestine. As it moves along the intestine, tiny bits of food are taken into your blood and carried around your body to give it energy.

3 The parts of the food that your body does not want, or cannot use, are pushed along to the colon at the end of your intestine.

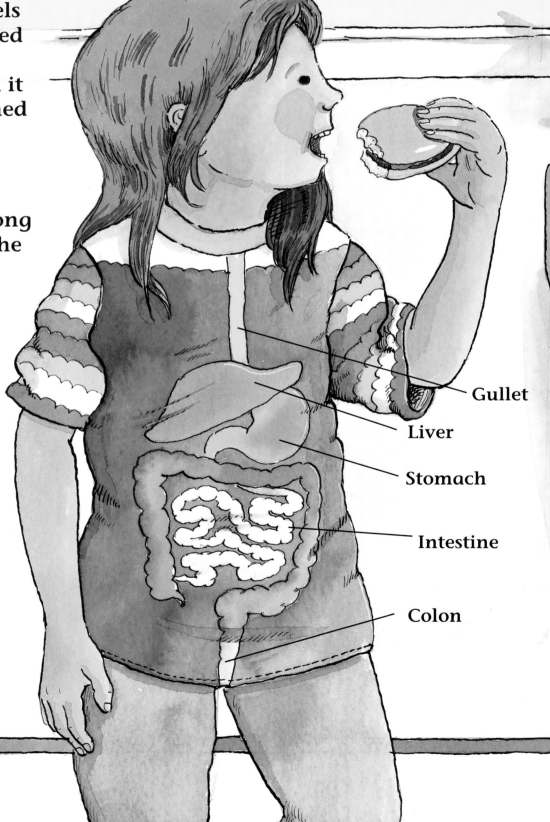

Gullet

Liver

Stomach

Intestine

Colon

When you burp, air rushes back up your gullet from your stomach. Fizzy, bubbly drinks can make people burp.

When you go to the bathroom, the waste food stored in your intestine passes out of your body through your bottom.

Burp

A meal can take up to three whole days to pass all the way through your body.

Kidneys

Rumble

Your kidneys help get rid of waste water, called urine, and your liver helps break down food.

When your stomach has been empty for a while, it may fill with gas and rumble. A rumbling stomach often means you're hungry!

21

My teeth

Going to the dentist is very important. The dentist helps keep your teeth and gums healthy. You need healthy teeth and gums to slice and chew your food so you can swallow it.

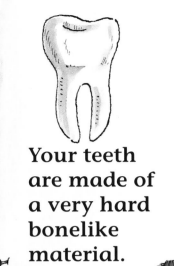

Your teeth are made of a very hard bonelike material.

Caring for your teeth

It is important to brush your teeth every morning and evening, as well as after meals.

If you do not brush away the tiny bits of food that collect on and around your teeth, your teeth may rot or decay.

The story of teeth
Our teeth change as we get older.

1 When you are born you have no teeth at all, just hard gums.

2 By the time you are two, you have about 20 teeth, called baby, or milk, teeth.

3 When you are about six, your baby teeth fall out. Larger, adult teeth grow underneath.

Kinds of teeth

Sharp incisors are for cutting food.

Pointed canines are for tearing.

Big molars are used for grinding and crushing.

Sometimes, as your adult teeth grow, they become crooked. You may have to visit an orthodontist, who will put braces on them to straighten them.

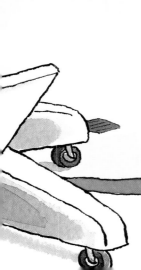

23

When I am sick

There are times when you feel sick. Maybe you have a stomachache, a cough, or an itchy rash. Sometimes you are sick because germs have gotten inside your body. So a visit to the doctor, and some medicine, will help.

Fighting germs

Germs are tiny living things that float in the air and in water. They are sometimes found in food, too!

Some germs can make you sick. Special cells in your body fight and kill germs.

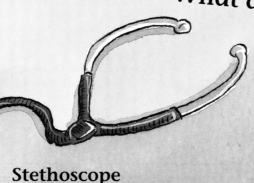

Things that help the doctor
What does a doctor use these for?

Stethoscope   Flashlight   Thermometer

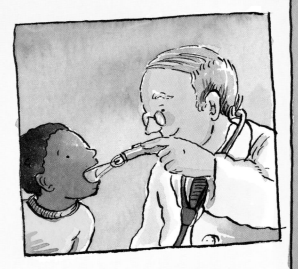

1 The doctor may take your temperature with a thermometer to find out how hot you are.

2 The doctor might listen to your heart and chest through a stethoscope.

3 Sometimes the doctor looks into your ears and throat with a special flashlight.

Some diseases, such as chickenpox and mumps, are very easy to catch, but you usually only catch them once. After that, your body learns how to protect itself against them.

Sometimes you are given a shot so you don't get sick. No one likes getting shots because they sting, but it doesn't hurt for long.

Staying healthy

Your body needs your help to keep it fit and healthy. Eating nutritious food, drinking lots of water, exercising, and getting plenty of sleep will all help you grow big and strong.

Exercise makes your bones, joints, and muscles strong. It is also good for your heart and lungs.

Food gives you energy. There are different groups of food, and you should eat food from each group every day.

Your body needs lots of water to help it stay clean on the inside, and to keep it working properly.

Keeping clean

It's important to keep your body clean, because washing helps get rid of germs.

Wash your hands before you eat.

Take a shower or bath every day.

Wash your hair to keep it shiny and healthy.

Proteins build strong muscles and bones. We get protein from meat, fish, cheese, and milk.

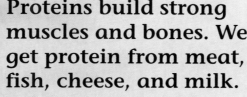

Fiber helps you digest your food. Fiber comes from fruit, vegetables, cereal, and rice.

Fats store energy for your body to use. Fats come from milk, cheese, and meat.

Carbohydrates give your body energy. They come from bread, cereal, rice, and pasta.

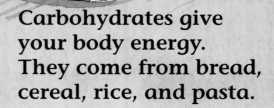

Where I came from

Every person in the world begins life as a tiny baby. Before you were born, you grew inside your mother's body in a warm, watery place called the uterus. After nine months you were ready to be born.

Sometimes, moms have more than one baby growing inside them. Two babies are called twins.

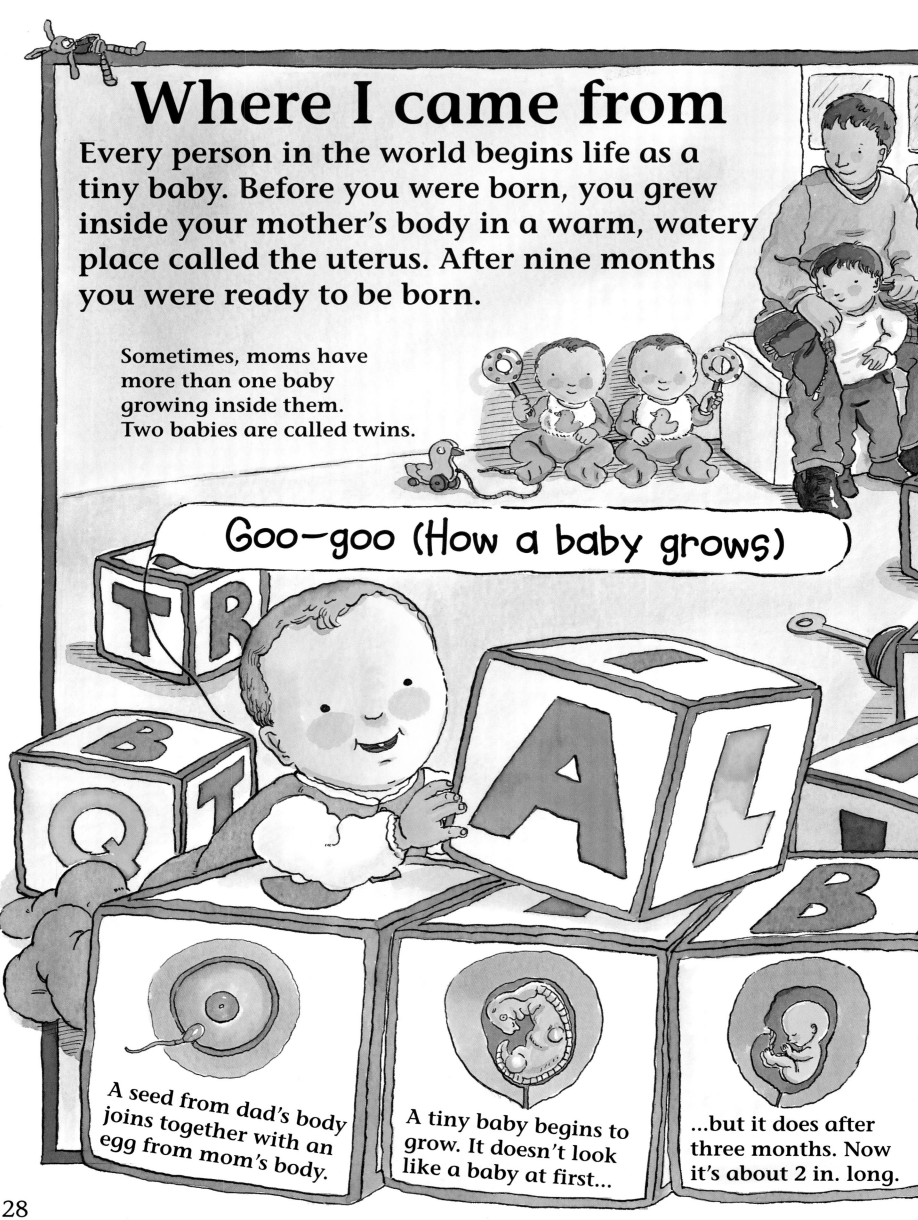

Goo-goo (How a baby grows)

A seed from dad's body joins together with an egg from mom's body.

A tiny baby begins to grow. It doesn't look like a baby at first...

...but it does after three months. Now it's about 2 in. long.

Inside the uterus, babies get all the food and oxygen they need through a cord called the umbilical cord. Your belly button shows you where YOUR cord was once joined to your stomach.

A mother's stomach grows bigger as the baby grows. It protects the baby, keeping it safe and warm.

At five months it starts to move around and begins to kick.

At six months it can suck its thumb and may get hiccups.

At nine months the baby turns upside down.

Growing up

From the moment you are born, until you become a teenager, your body slowly grows and changes.

When you were a brand-new baby, you couldn't do much and needed lots of care.

When you were just a few months old, you probably began to sit up and crawl.

When you were about one, you probably learned how to stand up and began to toddle.

By the time you were three, you could probably run, skip, hop, and jump.

Most children go to school when they are five years old. Going to school is a very exciting and important part of growing up.

Just before you become a teenager, when you are about twelve years old, you will notice that your body begins to change.

By the time you become a teenager, you will be taller and heavier. At around eighteen, your body will stop growing, but there will always be new and exciting things to do and learn.

Index

A
Ankle 3, 7
Arm 3, 6, 7
Artery 9

B
Baby 28, 29, 30
Baby tooth 23
Backbone 6, 7
Balance 11, 15
Belly button 2, 9, 29
Blood 8, 9, 20
Blood vessel 9
Bone 6, 7, 15, 26
Brain 6, 10, 11
Breathing 8, 9
Burping 21

C
Canine 23
Cheek 2
Chest 2, 8, 9, 27
Chickenpox 25
Colon 20

D
Dentist 22, 23
Disease 24, 25
Doctor 25

E
Ear 2, 14, 15
Eardrum 15
Elbow 2, 7
Energy 26, 27
Exercise 5, 26
Eye 2, 16–17
Eyebrow 2, 6, 17
Eyelash 17
Eyelid 17

F
Fats 27
Fiber 27
Finger 3
Fingerprint 13
Food 5, 9, 20, 25, 26, 27,
Foot 3, 7

G
Germ 9, 12, 24, 27
Glasses 17
Gullet 20, 21
Gum 22, 23

H
Hair 2, 4, 12
Hand 3, 4, 7
Head 3, 10, 12
Hearing 11, 14–15
Heart 8, 9, 26
Heartbeat 8
Hips 3, 7, 9

I
Incisor 23
Intestine 20
Iris 17

J
Joint 7, 26

K
Kidney 21
Knee 3, 7

L
Leg 3, 6
Lens 17
Liver 21
Lung 8, 9, 26

M
Medicine 24
Memory 10, 11
Milk tooth 23
Molar 23
Mouth 2
Mumps 25
Muscle 6, 7, 11, 26

N
Neck 3
Nerve 11, 13, 15, 16
Nose 2, 18, 19

O
Oxygen 8, 9, 29

P
Protein 27
Pupil 16, 17

R
Retina 16
Rib 7

S
Scab 13
Senses 14
Shin 2
Shoulder 2
Sickness 24, 25
Sight 11, 14, 16, 17
Skin 4, 12, 13
Skull 7, 10
Sleeping 5, 26
Smelling 11, 14, 18–19
Sneezing 8
Sound 14, 15
Stomach 2, 20, 21, 29

T
Talking 11
Taste 11, 14, 18, 19
Taste buds 18
Tear duct 17
Temperature 25
Tendons 6
Thigh 2
Toe 3
Tongue 18, 19
Tooth 22, 23
Touch 11, 14
Twin 28

U
Umbilical cord 29
Urine 21
Uterus 28, 29

V
Vein 9

W
Waist 3
Washing 27
Waste 21
Water 5, 21, 26
Windpipe 8, 9

Y
Yawning 8

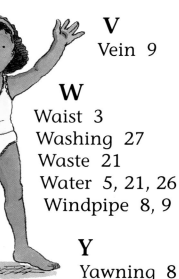